Mic

E. J. Schatz

SPURBOOKS LIMITED

Published by:
SPURBOOKS LTD
6 Parade Court
Bourne End
Buckinghamshire

© E. J. Schatz 1975

Maps reproduced from the Ordnance Survey by permission of the Comptroller of H.M. Stationery Office: Crown copyright reserved.

All Rights Reserved: No part of this publication may be reproduced, stored in a retrieval system, or transmitted in any form or by any means, electronic, photocpying, recording or otherwise, without the prior permission of the publisher.

I S B N 0 902875 95 7

At the time of publication all the walks in this book were made along paths designated as official footpaths, but it should be borne in mind that deviation orders may be made from time to time.

ACKNOWLEDGEMENT

Some of the material in this book has been previously published in the *Birmingham Evening Mail*, under *Week-end Walks*, and the Author and Publishers are grateful to the Editor for permission to draw on this.

ALSO IN THIS SERIES:

Contents

FOREWORD

If you have two loaves,
Sell one and buy a lily
— Chinese Proverb.

IN WRITING this book my hope is that the reader will look upon it as an investment—an investment in enjoyment.

The walks described in this book are but a pointer to what you can yourself, as you progress in the rambling game, discover. Get out the Ordnance Survey maps and study them. We have, in this country, the finest maps in the world—the Ordnance Survey Maps. With the metric scaled maps of 1:50,000 (First Series) used in this book, we have even more space to the mile. And, if you want something larger, we still have our 2½″-to-the-mile packed with detail. O.S. Map Sheet No.'s are given for every walk and the appropriate sheet should be taken with you each time.

Go to it, therefore. Try out my walks—in each case I have given a shorter alternative for those unable or unwilling to tackle the relatively easy distances of the full walk—and I'll wager that you will soon be planning your own routes, from the O.S. maps.

Some of the material in this book has been published in part in my *"Week-end Walks"* in the *Birmingham Evening Mail*, which have appeared for very many years each week and I am grateful to the Editor for permission to draw on this.

Oh, just one more thing. Should you be a little nervous of stepping out into the fascinating world of discovery of the countryside on your own two feet, join one or other of the many walking clubs which we have in the Midlands. You will learn from them and enjoy the jolly good company of both sexes and all ages—rambling knows no age limit, up or down —in so doing. Finally, think of others and remember the Country Code.

See you on a fieldpath, sometime.

E.J.S.

Summer, 1975.

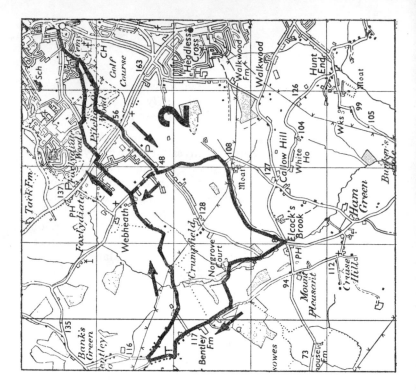

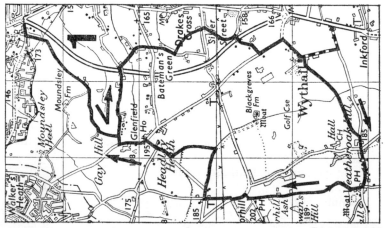

Crown copyright

ON THE BOUNDARY OF BIRMINGHAM

From City Centre by No. 48 or 50 bus to Maypole Terminus. Refreshments at Wythall or Coach and Horses Inn, Weatheroak Hill.

As THIS book is all about walks around the Midland area, let us start with one that actually commences at Birmingham city boundary and can be reached easily from the city centre by buses Nos. 48 and 50 both of which run to the Maypole terminus where our walk starts.

Taking Druids Lane from the grassed roundabout on A435, the first lane on the left is Crabmill Lane. In my opinion, this is one of the prettiest lanes in, or about, Birmingham. There is a scatter of houses as it leaves the boundary but nothing else along its length save a cottage and a couple of farms. In front of one of these, Yew Tree Farm, the land drops away affording fine views over the countryside.

Along here I came on a golden summer afternoon, the sun dappling the lane surface through the overhanging branches and, reaching Dark Lane, swung left to pass Crabtree Farm, its great barn once a bakery.

Pass over the motor road past Chapel Cottage where, long ago the Unitarians met before they built their charming chapel and manse, much higher up the lane, the high bridge drops you at Baccabox Lane leading off right. This name has nothing to do with the noble weed since it is said to have got the title from a box hedge—"back of the box."

Crossing Bateman's Lane, past Holly Farm, look out for a gate in the left hedge which leads into the considerable and pleasant expanse of Wythall Park, an excellent spot for a picnic and a rest.

From the car park here, cross Silver Street to Wilmore Lane to again swing by a high bridge over the motor road and pass the once-moated Wythwood Farm. The name is a relic of an earlier designation of Wythall—Withanwoerthan, recorded in a land charter of 849 A.D. It means "the enclosure where the withies (oziers) grow."

Out on Middle Lane and left, follow Chapel Lane off right. Here stood the pre-Reformation chapel of Wytho and Sheldon records it on one of his famous tapestry maps. In 1862 the new Church of St. Mary was completed, built largely of red brick, with its high campanile tower, rather different to our general heritage of churches.

The lane bends past the church and passes the former tiny church school to reach a fine, half-timbered farm. If you now wish to cut your walk short, continue straight ahead to pick up the lane off left which will drop you on A435 where a bus may be caught back to the city boundary at the Maypole. You will then have walked a little over 4 miles.

But to make a splendid round trip of 9 miles, take the public right-of-way pointing through the farmyard and, bearing half left across the meadows and passing a pond where you make for a battered stile beside the brook. The plank footbridge is broken but there is only a trickle of water and it is not difficult to cross and climb up the bank.

Then over meadows to the farm on the right and once through the gate where the public footpath sign points, you are out on Hill Lane where the contour is 588 feet above sea level. Along this to the right, Weatheroak Hill is reached and the views from this vantage point cannot be bettered.

Dropping down the steep hill, the old Coach and Horses Inn at the bottom, as it guards the corner of the Roman Ryknild Street, dispenses nourishment.

Now follow this narrow and deep route, rich in natural history and overhung with trees, passing scattered farms, until another old inn, the Peacock, is reached. Go along Clewshaw Lane and right by the way signposted to Kings Norton. Right again along Bell Green Lane, continue straight ahead by the bridleway and, where is branches left, along a muddy track known locally as Old Lane, follow this to return to Bell Green Lane.

Right along here and take the left turn at the crossways to Dark Lane and Crabmill Lane for the return via Druids Lane to the Maypole bus terminus.

AROUND REDDITCH

From Birmingham by Bus X7, or 147, or by train. Refreshments in Redditch or the Brook Inn.

LE RED DYCH, as it was known in 1300 A.D., is now the thriving town of Redditch with a great sports complex, including a ski-run; a modern shopping centre and a bus and railway station which enables it to be reached within the hour by bus (nos. X7 or 147) or train from Birmingham.

It is worth the trip for, around the town, is delightful Worcestershire countryside with many footpaths, mostly easy to follow and signposted.

Until the early 19th century, Redditch remained small and it was then that the water power of its river, the Arrow, began to be developed for the manufacture of needles and fish-hooks. Before the Reformation it leaned heavily on the great Cistercian Abbey of Bordesley, about a mile north, founded by the Empress Matilda in 1136, which has now almost entirely disappeared, although current excavations are revealing many interesting remains.

From the bus and railway stations, at the bottom of Unicorn Hill, take Bromsgrove Road and, opposite Redditch Football Ground, a public right-of-way sign indicates a footpath. Along here the town is left behind in minutes and a wide expanse of woodland, dells, glades and clearings, owned by the town and covering some 50 acres, can be explored. Known as Pitcher Oak Woods, it was once part of the great Feckenham Forest. Once there, bear half right.

There are several paths out of the woodland but aim to come out on the A448 at the spot where Heathfield Road for Webheath runs off opposite and, leaving the houses behind at the crossways, swing left to drop down Callow Hill into an entrancing contoured countryside.

If you want to shorten this walk to about 3½ miles, you should swing right to pick up the fieldpath back to the A448 and into Redditch which is described later in this walk.

Opposite the entrance to Redditch Golf Course, take the

lane off right to pick up the signposted public footpath to Elcock's Brook. The path runs over the cattle grid but leave it before the bridge leading into the farmyard, as the right-of-way follows the right bank of the stream as it meanders through the valley. This is a lovely fieldpath, easy to follow and typical of the fertile Worcestershire countryside.

Near where the path devolves on the lane, the old Brook Inn stands waiting to dispense nourishment to the traveller.

After a pause on the bridge, I followed the lane signposted to Webheath, the brook running on my left.

Where the lane takes a sharp bend, follow the signposted right-of-way over the cattle grid and along the drive to Norgrove Court where this lovely building with its twin lakes, fed by the brook, is graced by a back-cloth of trees. Swing left before the Court and the track is easy to follow and leads into lovely countryside.

Out on the lane swing right to pass the Bentley Farm with its half-timbering and narrow, Elizabethan red brick. Continue straight ahead to Upper Bentley which has more half-timbering and some delightful Jacobean chimneys.

Taking the lane signposted to Webheath, you at once strike off right and, where this lane bends, an ancient track, from which motorists are forbidden, is the route to follow. Obviously it was once a route of some importance for it has sunk deep beneath the fields under the countless passings of man and cattle, until it is now a rough and narrow way, and a joy for walkers.

Where the brook crosses the way, a footbridge will keep you dry but here is an ideal spot at which to linger so why not sit on the bridge and watch the rare "column dance" of the gnats, which only happens when conditions are just right, over the waters and the fishes, busy about their business among the bottom pebbles.

This way is known locally as Pumphouse Lane and it later becomes more of a lane and less of a track although it is always too narrow for vehicles to pass. Follow it straight ahead to the crossways and, opposite, a fieldpath sign points to Redditch and, via a new estate, runs into the A448.

Cross the main road for the road leading off opposite and,

very soon, the track enters Pitcher Oak Wood where various routes can be taken through the trees to Bromsgrove Road and Redditch where meals can be had before we return to Birmingham after 8 glorious miles afoot.

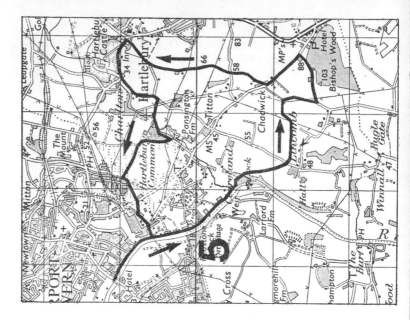

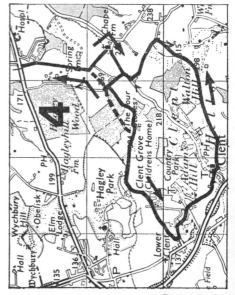

Crown copyright

THE LICKEY HILLS

By 62 bus from Birmingham Centre to Rednal Terminus (30 mins.). Refreshments at Rose Hill, or Rednal.

THE LICKEY HILLS are perfect on a winter's day and make a splendid walking area for that season or, come to think of it, for any season.

Midland folk are singularly lucky in possessing this wide area of hills, woodland and glens relatively close to Birmingham city boundary and in Worcestershire. They were once part of the Bailiwick of Bromsgrove and can be reached by bus No. 62 from the centre of Birmingham in 30 minutes. They are ideal for short walks as well as long ones.

Book to Rednal Terminus and if you are anxious to get on the hills, take the track opposite the terminus and, where it ends, continue climbing straight ahead to the ridge of the hills. All things were mantled in a winter's day mist and the vapour, condensing on the tree branches, plopped gently on my head as I strode through the woodland.

From the ridge, the golf course stretches below and, should you wish to be daring and descend to it quickly, the steep drop alongside iron railings (to which you can cling if you are nervous) is just the thing. For the less adventurous, continue right along the ridge and spiral more gently down via paths through the bilberries and bracken.

Strike across the golf course to a belt of woodland, where one can often see more squirrels, disappearing like grey ghosts into the tree tops. Then climb steadily via well-defined tracks to the trig point on the summit of Beacon Hill. Clear weather will give you splendid views and the topograph there will help you to pin-point local landmarks.

Bear left to the car park and here, should you wish to cut your walk down to about 4 miles, strike off left and meander through the pine woods to Rose Hill and thence back to the bus terminus.

To make a splendid walk of about 8 miles, cross the lane by the car park and locate the National Trust fieldpath sign directing to Beacon Lane. This is a fine path and, with its stout stiles, easy to follow. It drops on to the lane and, beside Beacon Farm, another sign points to a quiet and lovely path through a magnificent tree-scape. Nestling at the foot of the hill is a simple stone seat erected to Alderman Jack Wood, a great rambling writer, who died in 1969.

Out past a house and along a drive, the right-of-way runs on to reach the old Worcester Road. There, turn right through a wicket gate for a path alongside the new Worcester Road, the A38, and you come to a lay-by. This is one of the prettiest spots around the Midlands and is still relatively close to the outskirts of Birmingham.

You will now have to put up with the roar of traffic, for this is a busy route, but not for long because, once under the bridge carrying a road, you can climb up the grassy bank to a quiet track. Here no cars can pass and the going is satisfying.

Eventually you come out onto a lane, and cross straight over for the tracks spiralling up the lower slopes of Beacon Hill. Climbing to the summit, you are now 987 feet above sea level. Enter the pine woods, near the car park, as I have described earlier for the shorter route, and you can walk on a veritable carpet of fallen pine needles. Bearing right and dropping down steadily, you cross the brook and turn left along its course, which will bring you to a succession of pools which feed into the sizeable lake at Rose Hill where water fowl are always to be found.

A meal can be had at the golfer's cafe at Rose Hill or there are other places in Rednal before you return to Birmingham, but first cross the B4096 and the footbridge spanning the stream which runs alongside it and climb up Bilberry Hill to walk the ridge towards Kendal End. Where the hill ends, swing round, to return by the lower slopes, picking up the bridleway back to Rose Hill and thence to Rednal to complete some 8 miles of walking.

THE CLENT HILLS

By car or Midland Red 133 to Lutley Lane. Refreshments at Clent or the Vine Inn.

CLENT—the word comes from the Vikings and means "craggy"—sits at the foot of a delightful range of hills each with its own peculiar charm. Loosely known as "the Clent Hills," each has its own name—Walton, Calcot, Adams etc. —and a pleasant day can be had wandering about their several heights and dipping into the valleys.

There are facilities for parking, although somewhat limited, and the hills can be reached within a short time from Birmingham by Midland Red buses. There is a frequent service. The hills are equally easily accessible from the various other Midland towns such as Wolverhampton, Dudley, West Bromwich, Halesowen, or Bromsgrove.

One of my favourite approaches is to take the Midland Red bus No. 133 from Birmingham and book to Lutley Lane, Hayley Green on A456. Opposite Lutley Lane you will find a public right-of-way sign and a stout stile. Then follows a gentle climb up the grassy meadows. Make for an old sandstone barn and, keeping on, you will find a stile leading into the churchyard of the old and interesting church of St. Kenelm.

The whole district is thought to have been a place of some importance in Anglo-Saxon times and a palace of the Mercian kings once stood hereabouts. Nearby Uffmoor Wood is claimed to have got its name from King Offa. And here, where the church now stands, the young boy king, Kenelm, son of Kenulf of Mercia—he was only eight years old when he ascended the throne—was murdered by his sister, Quendreda, who poor lass, suffered terribly for her crime for legend has it that her eyes dropped out on her psalter.

The district was called Cowbatch, meaning the meadow of the cow. The boy's body was buried and when it was later discovered by miraculous means and dug up, a well sprang forth with curative powers, especially for eyes, and the place became a centre of pilgrimage. So much so that a village sprang up called Kenelmstowe. After the Reformation, the place fell into ruin and now hardly a trace remains.

A stained glass window in the church tells the full story in pictures and, on the south wall of the church outside, is a crude Saxon carving of St. Kenelm. The tympanum (stone arch over the door) is also said to be Saxon but is more probably Norman.

On the lane and to our right, we take the first lane right again which is Hagley Wood Lane, and, at the brow of the 1-in-7 hill, leave the lane for the steep climb up the tree-roots on to the hills and come to *The Four Stones* at the top. These look for all the world like ancient megaliths but were actually erected by one of the Lord Lyttletons to enhance his view from the ancestral home in the valley, Hagley Hall.

Now, if you wish to cut the walk short, drop down right into the valley, returning to Hagley Wood Lane by the lower paths, climb the stile opposite and link up with the fieldpath by which we came to return to Hayley Green. This will have taken you 3½ miles.

But, for a sparkling day's walk of almost 8 miles, continue from the stones to drop gently through the bracken to the boundary of Hagley Hall Park for a bridleway which will afford fine views of the many magnificent trees in the Park. You will also see the "ruined monastery" which is not old and has never been a monastery but was another erection by the Lyttletons to improve their Park.

Out near a pool, the foothills have now to be climbed to swing right and drop down to the hamlet of Lower Clent, coming out on the lane below Adams Hill. Follow it to your left, picking up the little stream which will accompany you into the village of Clent where meals can be obtained at a cafe or at the Vine Inn, a little way up Vine Lane.

Here is another splendid church, dedicated to St. Leonard, Patron Saint of Prisoners, with his sign of broken fetters. A priest is recorded as having served here in 1199 A.D. The church is built on several levels and the flint east window in the chancel looks out onto the trees and the hillside.

A track runs beside the churchyard on to Walton Hill where there is a splendid walk all along its ridge and where there will be many temptations to pause and gaze far over the "coloured counties."

Dropping to the lane and making our way back to Hagley Wood Lane, we leave by the stile I have earlier described to connect with our footpath across the meadows and return to A456 at Hayley Green.

This round walk offers countless ideal picnic spots and is a splendid day out for the family that is fond of walking and a spot of climbing thrown in for good measure.

A RAMBLE FROM STOURPORT TO HARTLEBURY

By Midland Red 133 from Birmingham. Refreshments in Stourport.

FOR the family rambler a visit to a specific place of interest as the object of the ramble is great fun for youngsters. If it is to one of the County Museums then you will have to tailor your ramble to permit the visit and the Worcestershire County Museum at Hartlebury is just about the right size.

Situated near Stourport, it offers excellent value at a moderate price for adults, children, students and senior citizens. It is open Monday to Thursday from 10 a.m. to 6 p.m., Saturdays and Sundays, 2 p.m. to 6 p.m. The Museum has a picnic area, a nature trail and a splendid collection of caravans, old tradesmens' vehicles, old motor cycles, bicycles, a forge, a wheelwright's shop and other exhibits.

The attractions are housed in a part of the Palace of the Bishop of Worcester and include period rooms, old childrens' toys, ancient writing materials, tools, railway material and a lot more.

It is ideal as a club ramble, and can be reached from Birmingham on Midland Red bus No. 133 which is a half-hourly service from Birmingham. If you come by car, there is plenty of parking available at Stourport and the town itself is particularly attractive to youngsters as it has paddling pools, miniature golf, a fairground and provides river trips along the Severn.

You start by climbing down the spiral iron steps from the great bridge spanning the Severn and making your way along the river-side path to cross the canal which feeds into the Severn by the lock, and then cross the River Stour by the more substantial bridge.

Leaving the great Power Station behind us, we pass, on the opposite bank, the hermitage of Red Stone Rock and you can see, across the water, the many rooms, passages and chapel which the monks cut in the sandstone. Legend has it that the monks, at this bend in the Severn, rescued from the water unwanted babes which had been cast into the Severn higher up the river. Baptising them with the surname of "De la River", and church records in the district confirm such names, they brought them up as good Christians.

Reaching Lincomb Lock, which is a busy point in the Severn's boat traffic, for traffic lights control the flow up and down the river and, just past here, you leave the river-side path to climb up the sandstone cliff to reach a footpath high above the water, overlooking the weir.

Now follow up the fieldpath to emerge on the lane and cross over to a farm track near some silos. Bearing first right, the track is not difficult to follow and you should keep as your landfall the distant water tower which stands before Bishop's Wood. Out on the lane, follow this to your left, you come to the A4025 and walk left along this a little, to the first lane off on the right. This is a lovely narrow and quiet way, deeply sunk beneath the surrounding fields and lined with soft sandstone rock.

Go straight ahead at the crossways for more pleasant and quiet lanes and suddenly you arrive at Hartlebury, near the church. For 900 years a church has stood here, although the present one has been much restored. Part of the font is very old and the church has a pre-Reformation bell, possibly 550 years old. The scallop-shell motif, is an emblem of pilgrimage to the shrine of St. James at Compostella in Spain. Actually, this emblem also has pagan symbolism. Six Bishops lie buried in the churchyard, for Hartlebury is the home of the Bishop of Worcester and has been so since Burhed, King of Mercia, gave the Manor to Bishop Ealhun in 854 A.D. The County Museum can now be visited.

The Castle, protected by the moat, has witnessed much over the centuries and the present pleasing structure, largely rebuilt in the 18th century but incorporating much that is old, is a delight to behold. Somewhere hereabouts is an ancient oak, called the Mitre Oak, and is reputed to mark the very spot where St. Augustine assembled the Welsh Bishops in 603 A.D.

Hartlebury means the "hill of the harts (deer)" and it is pleasant to sit on the high wall, above the moat although, in my opinion, possibly the best view of the Castle and the moat is from the bend on B4193, which is the route to take after you have visited the Museum.

TO RETURN TO STOURPORT

At this bend, a lane leads off left to pass **Charlton Mill** and wind through narrow, bush-clad banks, to the crossways. Right here and over the brook, look out for white-painted posts through which you can enter Hartlebury Common and wander by whichever route you wish towards the power station. Following the sandy tracks over the Common, note the considerable depths of pure seaside sand everywhere, relic of millions of years ago when this land was under the sea.

Using the chimneys of the power station as your landfall, drop down to A4025—the main road bisects the Common—and, through head-high bracken in season, cross the road and follow the track back to the riverside walk to Stourport where meals can be had.

The complete route is about 7 miles but, should you wish to shorten to about 4 miles, then follow the *return* route both out and back.

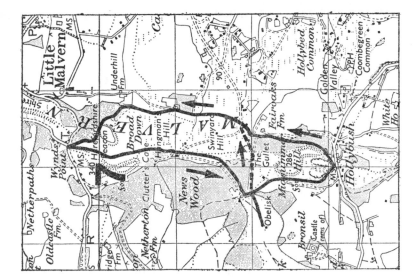

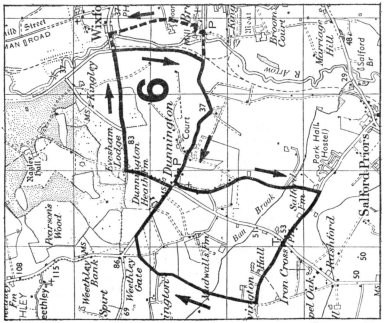

Crown copyright

AROUND WIXFORD

By Midland Red 148 to the Fish Inn, Wixford. Refreshments at Queens Head Inn, Iron Cross.

THIS CAN be an easy field path ramble of 2½ miles, never far from the River Arrow, or a charming and varied walk of almost 8 miles, both easy to follow. Our start is at Wixford and, while there is limited parking off the road, the village is on the route of Midland Red No. 148 bus from Birmingham which stops at the Fish Inn. Many fishermen get good sport along the banks of the recently widened and straightened River Arrow.

Go back over the bridge and then follow the course of the long-disused railway, opposite, where the road takes a sharp turn, a fieldpath starts, which initially follows the line of the old railway fencing and runs through quiet and scenic pastures.

All the way the Arrow lies on the left and, approaching what was once Broom Junction and is now a Warwickshire County Council Yard, veer slightly away for a stile on to the lane. This is where, if you wish to cut the walk short, you turn left and, over the Arrow and past the mill, bear left along the lane beside the mill and then right to look out for a stile and fieldpath passing Moor Hall and so you return to Wixford.

To cover the whole route, however, swing right from the Council Yard and follow the pleasant, twisting lane. Make for the beckoning fingers of 10 poplar trees on the skyline.

Soon you arrive at Dunnington, a charming village with a thatched post-office that is approached along a line of topiary work. The Church of England Primary School is a model of school construction in that it is solidly built of blue lias stone in Victorian Gothic style. It was erected in 1876 and looks likely to last for another century or so.

Taking the lane off left by the school signposted to Salford Priors you will avoid the traffic of the main road and also be able to enjoy the plum orchards on one side and the many colourful cottage gardens of which Dunnington can boast. Along here, too, is the church, likewise constructed in Victorian Gothic style and of similar stone.

Over the Ban Brook to the crossways where the great buildings of Park Hall, high walled, guard the corner. Swinging right, A435 is reached at Iron Cross and here, should you require nourishment, the Queen's Head Inn will oblige. Then, straight over the main road and follow the no-through-way signposted to Cock Bevington.

The lane runs through an avenue of horse chestnuts which, in season, provide a harvest of "conkers," and passes the Hall, clad in its creepers. By white cottages, a public footpath sign points off right and the track is easy to follow. Bevington Waste stretches far and wide on our left broken only by an occasional clump of trees and a cottage or barn.

A dell is reached, enclosed in trees and, keeping this on your right, make for a derelict stile in the hedge. Over this and straight ahead, one is out at Wood Bevington, a tiny hamlet of black-and-white thatched houses. We are now in fruit growing country where, in season the city motorist comes to indulge in fruit-picking, something that has become increasingly popular of late years.

Turn right on the lane until the A441 is reached and followed to the right. There is a good pavement, should you meet with any traffic. Where it reaches the A435, follow the latter to the left (again there is a sidewalk) skirting, where it bends, the extensive woods of Ragley Park. At the next bend, take the quiet lane straight ahead to fringe more woodland and return to Wixford.

Save time to explore this lovely village, for there is much to see, not least being the raised row of ancient cottages— now very much spruced up and refurbished—which were once part of a Throckmorton charity. The church, too, is a gem and can be reached either by a fieldpath beside the Fish Inn or a narrow lane further up the village.

Outside is a famous ancient yew, so old that its rheumy branches have to be supported on crutches. There is a small thatched "stable" in the churchyard where, long ago, the visiting priest left his horse while conducting service. Charming "pencil" windows are on the north side and there is a fine stained glass window to the Patron Saint, Milburga, prioress of Much Wenlock nunnery and a Saxon princess, daughter of Penda, King of Mercia, in the seventh century. An accompanying window represents St. Christopher, Patron Saint of Ramblers.

Situated on the course of the Roman Ryknild Street, it is more than likely that a much earlier church once stood here but there is still much Norman and 13th and 14th century work to be found. The south door is Norman and, in the south chapel is the great altar tomb of Thomas de Cruwe and his wife, Juliana, clad in the armour and dress of their times. This beautiful, life-size brass on the tomb is much sought after for brass-rubbing. A curious "badge" of a severed foot runs round the brass. There has been much speculation as to its meaning but, in my opinion, it may well be an emblem of the Crucifixion. This chapel was erected by Thomas Cruwe in 1411.

IN THE MALVERN HILLS

By car or coach to Wynds Point. Refreshments at Wynds Point.

LIKE A MINIATURE Pennine Range, the Malvern Hills guard
the border land between Worcestershire and Herefordshire.
They provide an invigorating walk of almost 10 miles along
the ridge from the North to Midsummer Hill's extremity.

This is an easier walk of the southern—and often quieter—
part and is ideal for a family or group outing by car or coach
for there is excellent parking available from the starting
place at Wynds Point where are also a cafe and an inn.

Just how these ancient rocks, constituting much of the
range, gained their name of The Malverns, is not certain but
I consider that it probably comes from the Celtic *Moel-Vern*
meaning the hill in the plain. Once a Royal forest—only the
King could own a hunting forest—the area became known as
Malvern Chase after Edward I gave it to Gilbert de Clare.
In those days the Chase extended for some 20 miles.

Leaving the Wynds Point car park, we climb the well-
defined path to the summit of Herefordshire Beacon, better
known as *British Camp* from what is probably the best
example of such a fortification left in all England. The
Beacon tops 1114 feet, and British Camp, on its summit is
thought to have been constructed in the 4th century B.C.

Legend has it that Caractacus, the great British Chieftain,
made a stand here and it would seem that the camp was
occupied later by Rome. Anyway, nearby, over a century ago
a considerable hoard of Roman coins was discovered. Just
to keep up the historic link, in 1650 a beautiful gold torque
was also found, probably of Anglo-Saxon origin.

Having examined the camp, we bear off across the hill to
successively drop and climb the well-defined tracks and, on
Hangman's Hill, the name is a relic of the days of the harsh
laws on the Chase, we can examine Clutter's Cave, cut in the
rock. This is said to have once housed a hermit and later
probably afforded welcome shelter for the hill shepherds.

Continue along tracks easy to follow, on the lower slopes

of Swinyard Hill, again an interesting name, from the times when swine were fed on the forest floor. Swinging right with News Wood over to our right, we enter Gullet Wood and follow the path to where, through a gate, a public right-of-way enters Eastnor Park. Climb to the hill topped by the Obelisk, for here is one of the finest spots for a picnic, and you may glimpse the herd of deer in Eastnor Park.

Just why past generations felt compelled to "improve" vantage points with monuments has always been a mystery to me but this great "needle" of stone pierces the sky in memory of Colonel Cox, son of Earl Somers.

Back to the gate and a steady climb up the grassy approaches of Midsummer Hill with, below us to the right, the faint earthworks of what was once Bronsil Castle and, on the summit, another hill fort which is periodically excavated.

There is a delightful legend told of Bronsil Castle. Erected about the 14th century and owned by the Beauchamps, the Lord of the castle set out for the Crusades. To ensure the safety of his treasure, he secretly buried it in the moat, appointing a raven to guard it. It is said by some that the raven is still there but, if so, he must be emulating Methusela in age for the treasure was never found. The knight promised that, should he not return alive from the Holy Land, his bones would be sent back and as soon as they were buried, the hiding place of the treasure would be disclosed to his heir. Unfortunately some of his bones, for he did not return alive, were lost and thus the whereabouts were never disclosed!

Bear left over Midsummer Hill and crossing part of the Red Earl's Dyke which was erected by Gilbert de Clare to define the boundary of his territory from that of the Bishop of Hereford with whom he was in dispute. This has seen fierce times, with Gilbert threatening to cut off the right hand of any of the Bishop's men whom he found chasing his deer.

Now we drop down to the wooded paths on the east side of Midsummer Hill to the lane. Had we continued over A438, the next hill is Ragged Stone Hill which also claims a legend, for a monk from nearby Little Malvern Priory was given a penance to climb this hill every day on his hands and knees. Understandably the poor fellow placed a curse on the hill whereby anyone on whom the shadow of the hill might fall would die. This happened to Cardinal Wolsey and history records his fate!

Just past the bend in the lane, a well-defined track leads past the quarry and this track is later left for paths over the foothills to drop to Castlemorton Common, a wide area of common grazing and a pleasant spot on which to laze on a summer's day. Here a long track follows the foothills to a pull up Tinker's Hill and passing the reservoir. Then to Wynds Point and the car park to complete our full walk.

To cut this down to 3 miles, it will be necessary to leave out Eastnor Park and Midsummer Hill and to make our way through The Gullet between Swynyard and Midsummer Hills to pick up the path skirting Castlemorton Common back to Wynds Point.

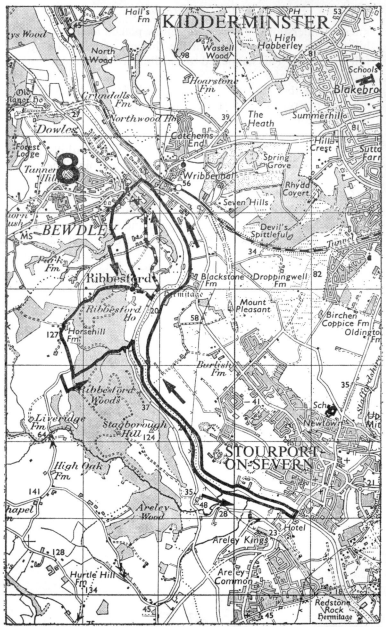

Crown copyright

A WALK BY THE SEVERN

By car or Midland Red to Bewdley. Refreshments in Stourport or Bewdley.

A FASCINATING place is Bewdley. The name, coming to us from the Normans, means "beautiful place" and Leland describes it: "The towne of Bewdeley is set on the syd of an hill . . . It risethe from Severne banke. . . . At the rysynge of the sunne from este the hole towne glitterithe. . . ." He said a lot more, all in praise of the place that the Normans built while the Saxon settlement on the opposite side of the Severn, retained the Saxon name of Wribbenhall.

Indeed, it would not be difficult to spend a whole day just roaming around the town, built on several levels and with the old quay and warehouses alongside the river, for it was once an important inland port where the hides and cloths from Wales, carried down the river in trows, were off-loaded for dispersal to the Midland towns.

And the names are fascinating. We have Lax Street, for example. Lax is a Norse word for salmon and, the river was always famous for fish. Fishermen from all over the Midlands make the journey to Bewdley.

Bewdley has a fascinating museum with many examples of old crafts, including a rope-walk. This alone is worth a visit to the town. There are pleasant walks, up and down the river and the vast area of the Wyre Forest sits at Bewdley's back door.

There is ample parking for those who must come by car and a good, fast Midland Red bus service runs from Birmingham.

Follow the road opposite the great church which, right in the centre of the town, effectively slows down incoming and outgoing traffic, and climb to Tickenhill Palace for the fieldpath which runs in front of the building.

Tickenhill was once the seat of the Marcher Lords and the house has seen more history than most. Built by Henry VII for his son, Prince Arthur, the young Prince was married by proxy here to Katherine of Aragon in 1501. Here, too, the young Prince's body lay shortly afterwards, on its way to Worcester for burial.

Easily followed fieldpaths giving from their rising contours fine views of Bewdley behind us, lead to a lane which is crossed for a track to Ribbesford where the fascinating old church always delights me.

The highlight of this historic church is the tympanum (archstone) over the door, preserved from the weather by the porch. The carvings on this tympanum have long been the source of conjecture and are generally considered to be that of a certain local hunter, Robert of Horsehill, who was shooting an arrow at a hind on the opposite bank of the Severn when an unfortunate salmon, at that moment, leapt from the water and was pierced by the arrow which continued on to kill the hind.

I incline, however, to a different version. The strange creature claimed to be a salmon, looks rather like a seal. Now, it is known that, in early times, the monks of Worcester pulled seals from the river and I take the view that this is meant to represent a seal.

Inside the church, which is dedicated to St. Leonard, is some ancient glass depicting St. George, a boar and a musical angel and there are quaint relics on the former rood screen, of faces with protruding tongues, pigs, geese and so on. There are three stone coffin lids which probably once covered dead Mortimers, for only the rich or important were buried in stone coffins and the Mortimers were extensive landowners in these parts. The church has one of the oldest bells in England, a 13th century casting.

Note the great house nearby, Ribbesford House. Long ago this belonged to the de Ribbesfords but, after becoming Crown property, it was given by King Charles to the Herberts.

Now taking the climbing path up the steep churchyard, we enter the woodland over a stile for a delightful shady walk to reach on a lane. Swinging left and passing Horsehill Farm, leave the lane at the corner for a right-of-way into Ribbesford Woods, passing a notice carrying caution against snakes!

Soon swinging left, we have a steady and interesting drop

through the woodland glades to come out beside the inn on B4194 and cross to pick up the riverside path to Stourport, a Severnside town much loved by holiday makers.

Crossing the great bridge which carries the A451 over the water, drop down to the opposite bank of the Severn and follow this to the left. This is another splendid riverside walk which, over stiles, skirts towering Blackstone Rock cut with the chapel and cells of the former hermits.

Eventually, via Wribbenhall, we reach Telford's great bridge, built in 1800 to replace the old bridge erected in 1447 and destroyed by floods in 1795. Over this, we are back at Bewdley, where meals can be obtained, to complete our full 8 miles.

If only a short walk is wanted, covering about 3 miles, after examining the Church of St. Leonard, Ribbesford, follow the farm track from the church down to B4194 and, swinging left, continue along this—it is a pleasant road, bordered on the right by the river—back to **Bewdley.**

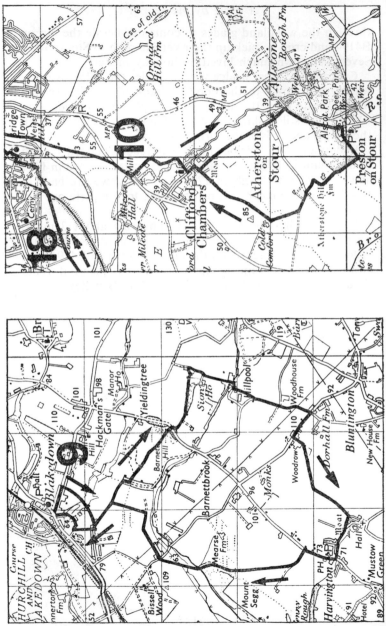

Crown copyright

TO HARVINGTON HALL, KIDDERMINSTER

From Birmingham by Midland Red to Blakedown. Refreshments at Harvington Hall.

THE PLACES of historic interest around the Midlands are legion. Many of these are open to the public on most days of the year and a rewarding hour or so can be spent discovering what they have to offer. Apart from this, they are often sited in areas of pleasant walking country so that the enjoyment of a ramble can be added. Such a place is Harvington Hall, near Kidderminster, of particular interest to my Catholic readers for it is here that St. John Wall, one of the last two English Martyrs, is supposed to have performed his priestly duties in the days of the Recusants.

I have been to Harvington many times, from all directions, for there is nothing better than to cross its moat—the Hall is moated all round—and leave the present world behind for a space, finishing the inspection of the Hall and its many priests' hiding places by taking tea there, before setting off for home.

This is one of my favourite rambles to Harvington. Frequent buses run from the Midland Red Bus Station in Birmingham to Blakedown on A456. If you must come by car, there is limited parking. By the way, the Old House at Home Inn at Blakedown has some old stocks behind the inn which are worth examining. Leave the main road by the B4188 and look out for the first fieldpath sign off right which leads to a remote route past the wide expanse of Wheatmill Pool to Wood Barn. Left along the lane, pick up the bridleway, just past a house, to steadily climb up Barnett Hill.

The path runs past the old quarry and drops suddenly to bring the walker out on the A450 which you cross over to reach the narrow lane opposite. Where this becomes a drive to Sion House, the route runs along a farm track to the left, passing later, through the farmyard, to strike a lane.

Follow this lane to the right and the charming hamlet of Hillpool is reached where one can lean over the bridge, listen to the chuckling of the waters and watch the fish in the clear brook. I once discussed with a resident of one of the cottages here the changing times and she told me of the days when £3 an acre was the price of good farm land and the cottages commanded a rent of 1s 6d per week. In those days the locals drew their washing water from the brook and their drinking water from a spring nearby.

Now follow the public right-of-way over the bridge, where the climbing track is composed of old discarded millstones and emerges, over a stile, opposite the school. Taking the lane to the left, we pass Woodhouse Farm and, at the cross ways, take the right hand turn and reach Woodrow. Look out for Woodbine Cottage for a track runs off here and becomes a fieldpath to Harvington Hall.

After an inspection of the Hall and the private chapel, a visit can be made to the nearby Catholic Church and then the moat is skirted by a fieldpath to come out in the village of Harvington on the A450, opposite the inn. A short way along the main road to the right a bridle way on the left is picked up and now follows a long and lovely walk through rolling countryside and bracken-clad slopes, spanning two brooks, to emerge on the lane near Bissell Wood. Cross over soon for the fieldpath off right leading down to Blakedown on the A456 to complete a total distance walked of 8 miles.

Should you want a shorter walk but still include a visit to Harvington Hall, then I suggest you follow the route I have shown as back to Blakedown, outwards, and return to Blakedown the same way. This will cut down the walking distance to 5 miles.

A CHURCH RAMBLE ROUND STRATFORD ON AVON

From Birmingham by Bus or train. Refreshments in Stratford.

THE ENJOYMENT of a ramble can often be increased by the many interesting things that can be seen en route. Even an elementary knowledge of geology, natural history, local history, or customs can put meaning and purpose into the countryside through which we walk.

One of the many "sidelines" to my rambles is an interest in our parish churches. We are lucky in having thousands of these, sometimes at the very heart of the villages which they serve, sometimes isolated by the decimations of the 14th century Black Death which totally wiped out the inhabitants of the village, leaving only the church standing. In England churches were built in that durable material, stone, a material which resists fire as a wooden construction does not.

So we are left with these old—often very old—places of worship which are also a "living museum" of the district in which they are found, where as often as not, past inhabitants are remembered as images carved in stone or inscribed in brass, wearing the armour or apparel of their times and, should you also have some knowledge of heraldry, you can learn a lot from the coats-of-arms on tombs or hatchments.

It is all very fascinating and this ramble will take us to a few of these parish churches all within easy reach of Stratford-upon-Avon, itself a place steeped in history.

There is an excellent bus or train service to Stratford, a town which, besides being the birthplace of the Bard, is of interest in its own right and very old. There was, indeed, a Roman settlement here where the Avon was fordable. The name comes from Anglo-Saxon *straet* simply meaning street and, of course, the termination of the word is obvious.

Another important matter which has added to Stratford's charm is the opening up of the 14 miles of approach canal from Birmingham by National Trust and the tireless work of Mr. Hutchings and his supporters in clearing and locking the Avon now make it navigable right through to the sea.

Once in Stratford make for the south bank of the Avon and follow the willow-lined path to pass the lock and, on the opposite side of the river, the great church where Shakespeare lies buried and pass through the white kissing-gate near the footbridge. Pass under the bridge, which once carried a railway, to swing left and follow the public fieldpath sign directing you to Clifford Chambers.

This will take you over high fields via Cross 'o-the-Hill and leads out to the A46. Follow this for a short way and then, near the Textile Mill, take the public right-of-way which leads by pleasant ways to the east bank of the River Stour. Most of the names of natural features such as rivers and mountains come from the Celtic tongue and the meaning has become lost in time but "Stour" means "strong".

Crossing the footbridge over the water, Clifford Chambers is reached and the church is well worth examination. It is thought that Shakespeare's mother stayed for a time at Clifford Chambers to avoid an attack of the Plague which raged in Stratford. There is a mass dial scratched on the church wall and the seven-sided font is thought to be Saxon.

Beside the church is what must be one of the most picturesque rectorys in the country, a veritable dream of "black-and-white" and wonderfully preserved.

At the end of the lane stands the Hall where, incidentally, in the grounds, the skeletons of monks have been discovered. Leave by the fieldpath running to the right of the Hall and beside it, you will find the way easy to follow. Make for the spire of the church ahead and you are eventually out, after following this delightful fieldpath, at Atherstone-on-Stour.

Here we have a splendid example of what is known as Victorian Gothic church architecture for this church was built only a century ago, replacing the former church. There was a great Gothic revival both in church building and ritual in Victorian times and it is sometimes difficult to distinguish between churches erected then and those of the 14th century. Only the font—probably Saxon—remains from the former church. The Winged Beasts of St. Mark and St. Luke, carved in stone, guard the chancel.

Follow the lane ahead, leave it at the bend before Alscot

Park for the fieldpath near a cottage and skirt the park to later enter it by the right-of-way, cross and come out through a narrow coppice by the farm on to the lane and Preston-on-Stour. On your way across the park you will obtain fine views of the Stour as it winds through the meadows.

The church, high on the mound, at Preston-on-Stour—incidentally the name of the river is pronounced locally "Stoor"—is approached through fine wrought iron gates. The interior is unusually Baroque in appearance, the chancel being mainly a memorial to the West family.

Here is a wealth of stained glass, some of it of Dutch origin and a great monument to Sir Nicholas Kempe is said to have been moved from a church in London by James West. Just how he managed to effect an unusual removal of a monument of this nature is anybody's guess.

Now take the gated road to Atherstone and climb into the skyline with magnificent views across the countryside to Meon Hill. Passing ancient Atherstone Hill Farm, the track passes through one of its gates but follow the farm track to the left and leave it, on the brow of the hill, for a fieldpath back to Clifford Chambers.

A fieldpath sign points to the west bank of the Stour where, at times, a heron can be spotted, and out on to the A46 for the return to Stratford over the fields by the way we left it earlier.

The total distance covers about 9 miles but this can be halved if you return from Clifford Chambers and follow the west bank of the Stour, as described above, leaving out Atherstone, Alscot Park and Preston-on-Stour.

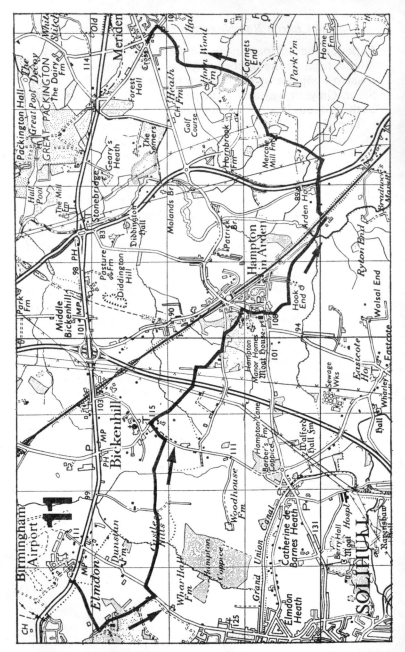

Crown copyright

A RAMBLE TO BICKENHILL

From Birmingham or Coventry by bus to Elmdon. Refreshments at Elmdon or Bickenhill.

ABOUT 55,000 acres of countryside are disappearing every year under the bricks, mortar, concrete and ashphalt of urban growth.

The building of the great Exhibition Halls at Bickenhill off A45, half way between Birmingham and Meriden, the reputed centre of England will undoubtedly be a commercial asset to the Midlands but, with every step forward, we leave something behind and, for those who regret this sealing up of the good earth in concrete, there is at least one consolation in that this development is all on the north side of the A45 so it is not likely to greatly upset the quiet charm of the ancient village of Bickenhill which, in the sixth century, was founded by the Saxon, Bica, giving the place its name—Bica's Hill.

Five hundred years later came the Normans and in the Domesday Book it records the place as belonging to Turchil, also a Saxon. How a Saxon, twenty years after the Norman Conquest, could still be in possession, presents an interesting problem to the historian. Evidently Turchil—who also owned several other manors—was something in the nature of a Quisling in his day.

The Birmingham Airport at Elmdon is easily reached by bus from Birmingham or from Coventry and, immediately over the high pedestrian bridge spanning A45, a public bridleway sign points into a wooded countryside.

Go straight ahead along the well-defined track, swing left to pass the charming little church of Elmdon, remote and trimly kept, and you are now in the old park of Elmdon Hall, the Hall itself having completely disappeared although the ancient trees which once surrounded it remain to delight us, especially when autumn paints the leaves of the hardwoods.

Eventually out on the lane, swing left and look out for the public footpath sign pointing off to the right. If you come this way in late autumn, the fallen acorns from the oaks will crunch beneath your feet. Over a stile, cross the Low Brook by a single plank footbridge and climb the rising meadows to Castle Hills Farm. This old building contains much of an earlier construction and, indeed, the place was once moated.

Coming out via the side of the farmyard, cross the farm road for the stile opposite with the word "Footpath" painted thereon so that you do not go astray. Over the wide meadows the path runs to span another brook by a plank bridge. Keep the needle spire of Bickenhill Church as your landmark and the path leads past a dell and across the cutting of a "new" road for a paved track on to the lane. Follow the lane to the left and you are soon on the outskirts of old Bickenhill.

Opposite and short left, a stile on the right hand side leads to a short "church" fieldpath and Bickenhill's lovely church with its needle spire flashing lights as a warning to aircraft in their approach to the airport. Do not miss an inspection of this ancient place of worship and, if locked, the key can be obtained from nearby Church Farm.

A golden sundial tells the hours on the ante-tower. Inside, parts of the south door and the arcade are Norman. The chancel was rebuilt around 1300 A.D. There is a lovely stone reredos and much else to be seen.

An unusual piece of stone carving can be seen—a cockatrice and a harpy, clad in tall 15th century headdresses.

Now retrace your steps a little and pass Rose Cottage for a short track which ends in a white stile beside steel gates. Over the stile to a further one and then a plank footbridge carries you over a brook. From the quiet pool over to the right one can often see a heron rise or a wedge of mallards. Bear across to the hedge on the left for a stile which points to a path alongside the right hedge, skirting ploughed land.

A short stretch of grassy track is entered and followed to the right for a stile in the left hedge. Skirting the hedge and left, a brook is reached and a plank footbridge will carry you over and, bearing right, a stile leads to a lane. Follow this to the left and cross the Shadow Brook where the lane is lined with fine and ancient trees. Look out for the public footpath sign and stile on the right and, via steel kissing gates, Hampton-in-Arden is reached.

Should you wish to cut this walk down to about 4½ miles, then the return to either Birmingham or Coventry can be made by rail from here for Hampton has a busy station and plenty of trains.

If Hampton is first to be explored, swing right after leaving the right-of-way to the fine church, sited high in the centre of the great churchyard. There is much to enjoy, including a modern rood loft, beautifully carved. Coloured shields adorn the walls and there is a heart tomb which is of Early English construction. There is a blocked Norman north door. Stone benches are built into the walls of the aisles, relic of the time when churches contained no pews, the service having to be followed standing or kneeling, for only the weak and infirm used these stone benches, "the weakest go to the wall" is an expression still used!

Opposite the church runs a rough road called Belle Vue Terrace, containing a few houses; follow this to a fieldpath sign pointing between the privet hedge on the left and the path, via several stiles, over meadows leads to the ancient packhorse bridge spanning the Blythe. For many centuries its great cutwaters have resisted the action of the river and this is a pleasant spot, a favourite for picnics.

Over the bridge, follow the lane which swings under the railway embankment and comes out on A452 where, straight over, another fieldpath sign points to the farm. Past this, swing left and, over a stream by plank bridge, you ultimately come to the surfaced way. Cross and follow the track to Mercot Mill Farm to later come out on the lane at Cornet's End where another fieldpath, over a stout stile, skirts the quarry and crosses a further brook and footbridge.

The path now runs over the fields, coming out at Meriden to complete a walk of almost 9 miles. Here frequent buses run to either Birmingham or Coventry.

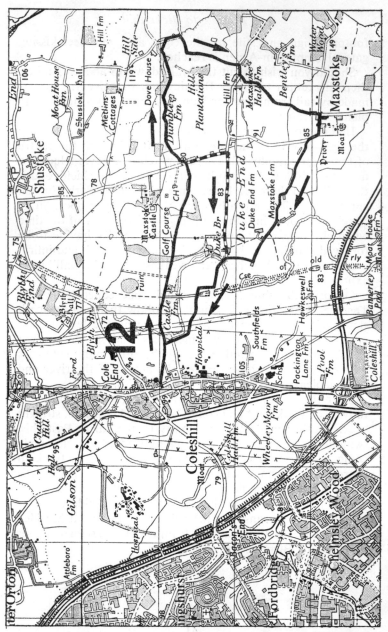

Crown copyright

FROM COLESHILL TO MAXSTOKE

From Birmingham by 161 or 171 Bus. Refreshments in Coleshill.

THIS WALK is packed with historical interest and, for good measure, will take you through some of the best Warwickshire scenery. It also has the advantage of being relatively close to Birmingham for 161 or 171 buses run a regular service to Coleshill, which is our starting place. If you come by car, ample parking is available.

Coleshill is old and was in being before our great Midland city. Indeed, at one time, Birmingham was known as "near Coleshill" and the place still retains much of the former charm. Here is still the whipping post, stocks and pillory combined, just as it was when rough justice was imposed and, as it was once an important stopping-place for stage coaches, there are several inns.

In 1346 Willelmus de Clynton was granted a licence to "crenellate" (build and fortify) a castle at nearby Maxstoke. This castle still stands, little altered, guarded by its moat. It is privately owned but we can admire it from close by, for a public right-of-way passes near.

Great builders were these De Clyntons for they also built Maxstoke's charming little church and the great Priory, which is now a farm, but with a massive gatehouse butting onto the lane, and a towering wall all round.

Let us pay a visit to all three and, in doing so, have an enjoyable and easy ramble.

Off the High Street in Coleshill, a lychgate, bearing inside a large-scale map of the local fieldpaths, leads to a walk to the great Church, large enough to act as a Cathedral, the towering spire of which often serves me as a landmark.

I must warn you that the church is sometimes locked, to counteract vandalism but, if you can get a look inside, this will be rewarding for it possesses a magnificent Norman font, thought to be the best example in all England. The "Rood" (or Crucifix) carving on one of the sides is one of the earliest sculptured representations left to us. Another probably represents St. Peter, others St. Mary Magdalene and so on. Note the holed impressions all round; these once held jewels before the Reformation. The font, as were many early Norman ones, is large enough for total immersion.

The church holds effigies of the de Clyntons, one on each side of the nave. They are in "founders" (wall) tombs. One of these has the crossed legs which supposedly denote a Crusader. The chancel, itself large enough to be a church, contains tombs of the Digby family.

A path runs diagonally across the church green to a steel kissing gate and a further one opposite and then out across the meadows to drop to the valley of the Blythe and a stile leading to a high footbridge over the river. Here, you will wish to pause and admire the riverside view. The river gets its name from an Old English word meaning pleasant, gentle, or merry.

Crossing the bridge, the track runs on, very easy to follow and passes Castle Farm with a wide duck pond where, on hot days, the cattle stand, belly deep, in the water. To our right the Blythe twists and turns, the whole presenting as pleasing a scene of pastoral England as one could wish.

The track ends at a gate to the golf course, but a stile on the right carries you over to a public right-of-way, skirting the course and passing between twin lakes usually alive with water fowl. The Castle lies over to the left.

To do the full ramble, you will have a walk of about 8 miles but, if you want to cut it short and include only Maxstoke Castle, swing right when you enter the lane from the golf course, then right again and follow the lane via Duke End and over the Blythe to return to Coleshill, making the distance some 4½ miles.

A stile in a hollow and a path alongside a strip of woodland leads to a further stile and a final one out into the lane. A little to the left and a track is picked up toward Dumble Farm. The footpath branches off before the farm for a stile and path again running beside the woods. Then make for rising ground ahead and a stile, the path leading across the meadow. Look out for the stile in the corner leading to a charming route through a dell where squirrels leap in the tree tops and, far below to our left, a little brook runs. At times one has to bend double beneath the leaning trees and, according to the season, all manner of woodland plants grow.

Out on the narrow lane over a footbridge of gnarled tree trunks, swing right, with the little brook for company. At the crossways, the lane on the right is taken, a quiet way offering extensive views particularly near a ruined barn. A wide vista of woods and pastures can be enjoyed and an even wider one when the summit of the climbing lane is reached.

At the next crossways, swing right and, near Hill Farm, a right-of-way runs across to Maxstoke Church. Should you fancy an easier lane route, swing left which will also take you to the church.

Maxstoke Church is mainly of 14th century structure with a fine east window and fragments of ancient glass. It has a surprisingly large number of hatchments (armorial boards). The custom was to hang these outside the houses on the death of a prominent person, the boards ultimately finding their way to the church. The word hatchment probably comes from "attainments." Skirting the churchyard and continuing down the lane is the great wall of the former Priory in an excellent state of preservation.

Down the lane is the gatehouse, a beautiful piece of work. The towering oak doors still hang on their wrought iron hinges and, through the archway, a glimpse can be had of what was part of the former Priory.

Now follow Arnolds Lane, using as your landfall the needle spire of Coleshill Church, three miles distant. Passing Frog-pond Cottage and over the Blythe by Duke Bridge, a short fieldpath on the right will connect you with our earlier field-path across the church green and back to Coleshill where refreshments can be obtained.

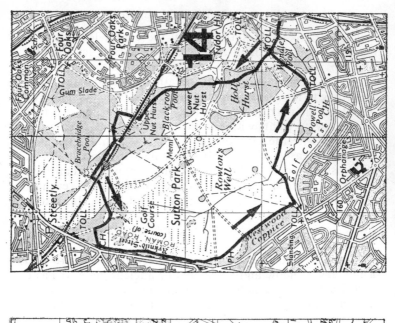

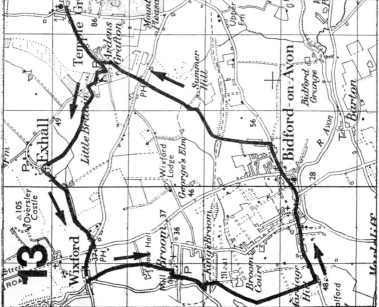

Crown copyright

FROM WIXFORD TO THE GRAFTONS

From Birmingham by 148 bus to the Fish Inn. Refreshments in Bidford.

ON THE B4085, where the hump-backed bridge over the newly channeled River Arrow will "lift your liver" if you take it at speed, lies Wixford—"Papist Wixford" according to the Shakespeare jingle—with a lovely little church, old as they make 'em. It can be readily reached by No. 148 bus from Birmingham or, if you must burn your own petrol, limited parking can be found.

Opposite the Fish Inn—its attractive sign leaves you in no doubt—a public footpath sign points into a coppice beside the river and carries you over a stout footbridge above the stream where a tributary feeds in, creating an attractive waterfall and the muted music of the waters.

Over another footbridge and a single plank spans a ditch.

The path continues to Broom, which Shakespeare dubbed "Beggarly." Take time to examine the village for it has much old property and the inn, appropriately carrying the sign of a *'besom'*—looks Elizabethan. The great mills of Adkins & Thomas churn out flower and feeding stuffs, the mill stream flowing beneath the building. Broom probably got its name from the gorse shrub which then covered the district.

Taking the signposted bridleway off King's Lane, with the river on the right, eventually you swing left to pick up a fieldpath running from a gate and crossing the long-dead railway line by farm bridge. This way passes near Broom Court with its stone shields, and continues over Marriage Hill where breathtaking views can be enjoyed.

The path reaches the A439 with Bidford a little to our left —"Drunken Bidford" according to Will's jingle. Here meals can be had and there is a pleasant parkland beside the Avon where one can sit. The river, now dredged and navigable, is often alive with boats.

In the side streets there is much lovely old stone property and the great bridge spans the Avon, no two arches alike, the stout cutwaters defying the current and the roadway still carrying traffic, after hundreds of years use. Bidford's great church is worth examination, perched high above the river and the Roman Ryknild Street nearby runs bang into the river, for this was where the Romans forded the water.

And here, if you want to cut your walk short, is where you can pick up the No. 148 bus back to Birmingham.

Just outside Bidford, off left, is Grafton Lane and, taking this, you are soon over the old railway line, and deep in fine, contoured countryside. On the brow of the 1-in-5 hill, pause to stand and stare, for the view is well worth the excuse to take a breather.

By the Golden Eagle Inn cross straight over for Ardens Grafton which Will Shakespeare called "Hungry Grafton." Here are a number of lovely cottages, mostly of blue lias stone. Then follow the lane to Temple Grafton.

Grafton, by the way, probably comes from the Anglo-Saxon *graef* (grove or thicket), the "ton" meaning a farmstead or settlement. Temple Grafton gets the word "Temple" from it once having belonged to the Knights Templar and, when the Templars were disbanded in 1312, it was handed over, as was much of their possessions, to the Knights of St. John Hospitaller. In Saxon times, the manor was owned by Evesham Abbey.

Back to Ardens Grafton, look for a passage off right in the centre of the village which will drop you on to the narrow lane. At the spot known as Little Britain, a long fieldpath runs off left to Exhall—Shakespeare's "Dodging Exhall"—near Glebe Farm and the extremely interesting little church with blocked Norman north door and several examples of ball-flower mouldings and much else.

Now follow the lane to the left for a pleasant finale to a good day's ramble, and then to Wixford.

AROUND SUTTON COLDFIELD

From Birmingham by frequent bus and train. Refreshments in Sutton Park.

> *Fill me a bottle of sack;*
> *Our soldiers shall march through;*
> *We'll to Sutton Coldfield tonight.*

GOOD BISHOP VESEY lies in his gracious chapel in the great church of Sutton Coldfield which, landscaped with lawns, rockery and flowers, presides over Sutton Coldfield. The chapel is carved with representations of the beasts and foliage to be found in the extensive Park which he obtained for the townsfolk in 1528.

Sutton Coldfield lies a little to the north of Birmingham and there is a frequent service of buses and trains which will get you there in a very short time. This, then, is an excellent ramble if you have not much time to spare for travelling or lf you wish to leave your car at home.

Miraculously, and because of the strict charters under which the Park was granted, it remains little changed from those historic days and offers a wonderful escape for Midland folk, right on their doorstep. The whole ramble described here covers some 7 miles but you can lengthen or shorten it at will by either entering the Park at a different gate—there are several—or cutting across it rather than following its perimeter as I have done.

The Park has several legends. In the old Arms of Sutton is a red rose. This comes about, it is said, from a hunt in the Park by Henry VIII. Suddenly a great wild boar turned on the King but, just as it was about to attack, an arrow shot by an unseen archer killed the animal. The King ordered that the person who had saved him from harm should be brought before him and discovered that it was a young and lovely maiden. Granting the maiden's request for the restitution of certain rights which had been taken from her parents, the King presented her with a red rose—now part of Sutton's emblem.

I usually enter by Wyndley Pool gate if, for no other reason, that there used to be a cafe here where I delighted to take meals and to watch the considerable flocks of water fowl on the pool outside. Here also is a car park should you come by car. This cafe is now closed but there are other pleasant eating places in the Park.

The waters of Wyndley Pool were mentioned by Leland in 1535 when they probably then acted as the fishpond of the Manor of the Earls of Warwick. Incidentally, there is a vast amount of water in the Park and we can enjoy some of this, scattered about the Park's 2,400 acres.

Cross the pleasant brook and you are in the Park precincts and walk straight ahead to Keeper's Pool via the glades of Holly Hurst. Hurst comes from Old English *hyrst*, a copse. It is hereabouts that there is a distribution of holly at Christmas time to Sutton folk. Keeper's is now a swimming pool but in the time of Henry VI, John Holte, Keeper of the Chase, kept fish there.

On into the glades of Lower Nuthurst, Blackroot Pool is skirted and left behind with Upper Nuthurst over to our left and what was once an earthwork of pre-history on our right.

Now under the railway line to Gum Slade—Old English *slaed* means a valley—and bear left to examine what is called the Druids Well. Just how it got its name, I do not know but, if it ever had any connection with Druidical times, then the Victorians erected a typical piece of work over it!

Round Bracebridge Pool where there is a cafe, are the "gathering grounds" spanned by many plank bridges and a surprising feeling of remoteness can be experienced here amid the trees. Now make for the railway line and the underpass track leading to the trees of Streetley Wood. Here is another entrance to the Park at Streetley Lodge.

Swinging left, we are skirting Sutton Golf Course and, off left again, we strike the rare remains of the Roman Ryknild Street. Sutton is lucky in possessing this relic of Roman times for it has been virtually untouched since it was laid down by the legionnaires. The area was probably boggy when the Romans came and the street is constructed of gravelly material, raised in the typical *foss* and *vallum*.

Toward Westwood Coppice and left, near Banner's Gate with the Municipal Golf Course on our right, Longmoor Pool is reached, followed by Powell's Pool. This wide expanse of water once provided the motive power for a mill forging agricultural tools. It is now the main boating pool.

Back at Wyndley you can pick up your car or make your way back to Sutton for bus or train to Birmingham.

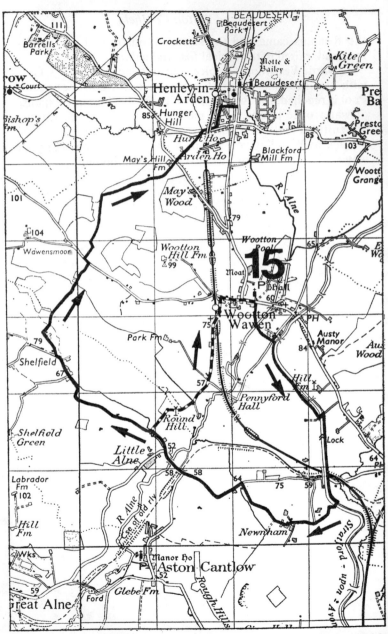

Crown copyright

FROM WOOTTON WAWEN

From Birmingham to Wootton Wawen by train or Midland Red 150. Refreshments at Henley in Arden.

THEY SAY that the great, grey church at Wootton Wawen, perched on the hill off the A34, is three churches in one, for it has at least three distinct parts. It is a fascinating place to visit and easy to reach from the Midlands, being served by rail and bus (Midland Red No. 150) from Birmingham. It is the centre of excellent walking country and the following is but one of the many routes which can be taken around this area.

But first, let us have a look at the church. Dedicated to St. Peter, in 1973 it celebrated its 1250th anniversary, for there was a church here in Saxon times and traces of Saxon building can be found in the north wall. Inside, under the tower, is as beautiful a relic of Saxon construction as can be found anywhere. This is the so-called Saxon Sanctuary and the "long-and-short" stone work of the Saxon builder is plain for all to see. The chained library in the church is unique and the charming wood carving on the parclose screens should not be missed.

See if you can find the small crosses cut in the stones of the porch. These, an old friend who lives in the district, informs me were cut by sons of the village on their safe return from service as sailors.

The name of the place is pure Anglo-Saxon; Wagen, the Saxon, friend of Leofric of Coventry and his lady, who has gone down in history as being the original strip-teaser, held the Manor. The rest of the word, Wootton, means "farmstead in the wood."

With the coming of the Normans, the manor was granted to the de Staffords, Tonei, of that family, occupying the place, and there was a monastery here, a branch of the great Abbey of Conches in Normandy. There are a number of half-timbered houses in Wootton Wawen, not the least picturesque being the old Bull Inn.

over the railway, road and stream below.

Reaching Draper Bridge, cross for the fieldpath to Newnham, a quiet, churchless hamlet with some charming cottages, through which run no roads of any importance. Ignore the public bridleway sign and continue straight ahead to follow the fieldpath sign off right, past the farm and, over quiet meadows, the lane is reached and we swing left along it, passing Aston Cantlow over to our left. These typical Warwickshire lanes are a delight to walk on and usually little traffic is encountered.

Over the Alne at a charming spot, to the B4089 but very soon, beside Pear Tree Cottage, turn left for the lane to Shelfield.

Take the first lane off right and, in spring, you will find the banks gay with bluebells, violets, wind-flowers and primroses. The lane climbs to pass The Poplars Farm with a great centre chimney set with brick shields. The lane soon becomes deep and narrow and the hedges, in season, carry many birds' nests.

Out at Wawensmoor and slightly left, to pick up the long and lovely fieldpath, to cross the stream by another newly-erected footbridge and enter the lane at Hunger Hill. Opposite, another footpath plunges under the railway embankment and we enter Henley-in-Arden by the back door.

Almost one mile long, the main street of Henley has every kind of architecture and an interesting church and cross. Here are a number of cafes and inns and the train or bus can take you back to Birmingham after a longish walk of almost 10 miles.

FOR THE 5 MILE WALK

To halve this ramble to about 5 miles, take the lane from Newnham to the lane just before the aqueduct and follow this to the left to cross the Alne and strike B4089 which is followed back to Wootton Wawen. This is a pleasant way offering some good views over the surrounding countryside.

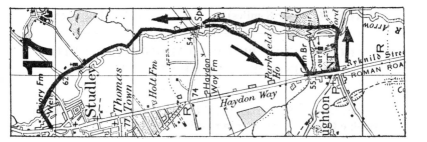

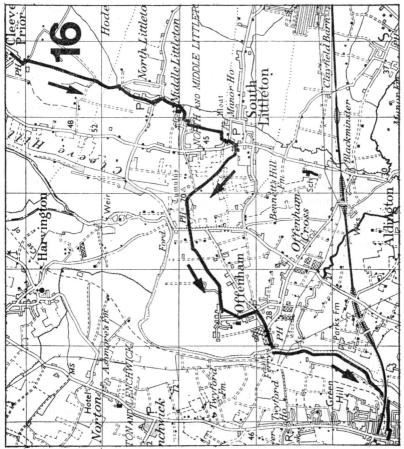

Crown copyright

FROM CLEEVE PRIOR TO MIDDLE LITTLETON
IN THE VALE OF EVESHAM

From Birmingham by No. 148 bus. Refreshments at the Bridge Inn, Offenham, or in Evesham.

IN MEDIEVAL times the income of a priest was provided by handing over a tithe, or tenth, of the produce of the land, although the priest often had also his own land, called the glebe, which he farmed himself. To house this tithe required a large building—a tithe barn—of which some examples still remain. These structures, particularly during Norman times, were really huge and they were then often the possession of the local Abbeys who had acquired the "livings" of the parishes.

One of the largest left to us is the tithe barn at Middle Littleton, built by Abbot Ombersley of Evesham in 1376 A.D. and it is a piece of artistry in golden Cotswold limestone.

The great, steep roof is tiled with split and graded limestone which, being somewhat porous, had to be laid thus to throw off the rain water.

Like many such barns built under Norman influence, the finials of the roof are like the carved prows of Viking ships for we must never forget that the cultured Normans—as their name implies—were originally Vikings who had settled in Normandy and picked up their better manners there. Indeed, in much early Norman architecture one can trace this Viking influence.

To see this great tithe barn, I strongly recommend this walk which, starting at Cleeve Prior–the No. 148 bus from Birmingham will drop you there—runs through some of the best and quietest of "orchard" country so, if you do it in the season of the fruit blossom, you will have this beauty as a bounty.

Cleeve Prior, with an ancient inn and a lovely old church and manor, plus many charming cottages, built mainly of blue lias stone and gardens gay with flowers, would take more space than this chapter to describe so let us be on our way by following the public footpath sign opposite the green, pointing to Littleton. It is easy to follow and, in all seasons of the year, rewarding to the botanist. When I came, the elder —the witches' tree—was in bloom. The word comes to us from Old Norse *eldre*, meaning the old folk. If you ever have to cut down an elder tree, always remember to tell it of the necessity to do so beforehand, if you wish to avoid bad luck!

Through the fertile plots of the Vale of Evesham, North Littleton is reached, a dream of stone, thatch and magpie buildings. Note the round, limestone dovecote. Then past the Ivy Inn to Middle Littleton with a trio of church, manor and tithe barn.

First let us look at the ancient, cruciform church with a preaching cross and an ancient yew of such girth that it has split and is "repaired" with a sheet of corrugated iron! The great Norman tub font, cut with designs and cable moulding, bears traces where the lock-hasps once kept the baptismal water from witches, have been cut out. A lovely stone surround is on the west wall and, in the north transept, there is a piscina with a credence "table" and encaustic tiles.

Then enjoy the manor and tithe barn, before leaving, by the signposted right-of-way through a kissing-gate opposite the church.

Four more kissing-gates and over the undulating furrows of the meadows, once medieval strip cultivation, South Littleton is reached. Here the post office is thatched and the great dormered manor house bears traces of construction over many periods. Here is another interesting church. Note, over the priest's door, carvings of an ass and a bishop. Inside is another Norman font, more encaustic tiles and old pews. Look for the recess behind the south door; this is to take a baulk of timber to act as a barricade. A primitive piscina or drain, which took the water from the washing of the Holy Vessels, probably from an older church, is in the chancel and an aumbry, or cupboard, where the Holy Vessels were kept, is lined with old tiles.

Beside the church runs a public bridleway. Where it bends right, continue along a narrow, dropping path and, as you emerge from the scrub growth, the wide beauty of the fertile Vale of Evesham is spread like a carpet before you.

Cross straight over the B4510 for a right-of-way threading through the growers' plots which ultimately brings you out at Offenham, by the great maypole. Continue to Ferry Lane, off right, to where this ends at the River Avon. Around here the bones of men and horses and odd pieces of armour have been discovered, relics of the defeat of Simon de Montfort at the Battle of Evesham on the opposite side of the river.

At Offenham, the name, of course, refers to Offa, King of Mercia—was the Court of the Abbots of Evesham and, at the manor, Abbot Lichfield, last Abbot of Evesham, ended his life after the Dissolution.

There is no bridge over the river so one has to call on mine host of the Bridge Inn who will ferry you across to the meadows of the opposite bank where, to the left, a lovely riverside walk awaits. Along here, in season, grow the "brandy bottles" of the water lilies and the tall spikes of purple loosestrife.

When the railway bridge is reached, leave the water and look out for the right-of-way sign which points an interesting fieldpath running beside the line right into Evesham.

Meals can be had in Evesham and the No. 148 bus picked up here for the return to Birmingham with, if you do the full walk, 8 interesting miles accomplished. Should you wish to shorten the walk to 3½ miles, follow the B4085 from South Littleton northward back to Cleeve Prior.

FROM STUDLEY TO COUGHTON COURT

By Midland Red from Birmingham. Refreshments at the Throckmorton Arms.

WHY THE River Arrow was so named was certainly not because its path was straight, for it twists and turns in a delightful fashion and, to follow its course, is the very negation of walking in measured ways.

There are a number of fieldpaths alongside the Arrow where the contented cattle graze and, if you tread quietly, as like as not you will see a coloured cock mallard escorting his drabber mate.

This ramble, easy to follow, takes us for most of the way with the Arrow for company and we start by following the public right-of-way sign off the A435 opposite the Inn as one enters Studley from Birmingham. Midland Red has an hourly service from Birmingham and there is also a good service from Redditch. If you come by car, some parking is available.

The path runs down the drive to Priory Farm. Once a priory of Augustinian canons, it was built by Peter de Corbucion in the 12th century. Much of the present building is the product of an extensive reconstruction in 1559 but it is not difficult to pick out parts of the old Priory. The Inn on the A435 opposite the start of the right-of-way is also old. Recently there has been some reconstruction and, during this, more than a ton of birds' nest were discovered under the roof!

Having admired what is left of the Priory, cross the Arrow by a footbridge and follow the bank, bearing across to the lane to enter it by a wicket gate. Now continue to the left, soon bearing right to pass the clearly-defined remains of the moat guarding the old Studley Castle of the Littletons. This lovely old building has now been divided into separate residences, each suite bearing the name of a Lord of the Manor who lived in the Castle.

Next to it stands the church and, as it contains much of interest, let us pay it a visit but first note the Saxon-like herringbone masonry in the north wall where is also the blocked Norman door. Most of the North doors are now blocked since they are no longer needed in the liturgy. The north side of a church was always, in pre-Reformation times, the devil's side and it was the custom, when a baptism was taking place, for the north door to be left slightly open so that the evil spirits, dispelled by baptism, could escape.

Inside can be found the remains of the rood loft steps. Under Elizabeth I, all rood lofts were ordered to be removed and very few remain except at remote churches but one can often find traces of the steps leading to the loft. The rood loft divided the chancel from the nave and was wide enough to hold a priest and his servers. From the rood loft the Gospel was read. Look for the stone carved with the Paschal Lamb. This is a sign of the Knights Templars and it is thus likely that this Order at one time owned land hereabouts. The altar rails come from Queen Anne's time and are the regulation width to keep dogs from the chancel! Here is a beautifully preserved stone coffin lid which once covered the body of one of the canons of the Priory. A Norman window of deep single splay still shows traces of wall painting.

Just past the church, the lane ends and, over a stile, the bank of the Arrow is reached. This riverside walk is popular with ramblers and is not difficult to follow. Soon, swinging slightly left, a feeding brook is spanned by a stile and footbridge and, with the river on our right, through a farmyard we reach the lane at Spernall.

Take the kissing-gate near the church and bear right to cross the Arrow by a new steel and concrete footbridge. Now the opposite bank of the river is followed to the left, and later, bearing right and away from the water, we come out on the A435 near the Throckmorton Arms where a ploughman's lunch can be obtained.

A short way down the main road and we are at Coughton Court, the ancient seat of the Throckmortons who are still in residence. The lovely castle-like place is in the care of National Trust and is packed with interest. Here is the chemise of Mary Queen of Scots, worn at her execution, the famous Throckmorton coat, which began as wool on the sheep's back in the morning, and was fully processed, woven, cut, and made up ready for wear before sunset. The place was once moated and the ladies of the house, it is said, did their fishing from the windows. The view from the top roof, which can be reached by spiral staircase, is captivating.

The grounds hold two churches, the ancient parish church and a lovely Catholic church, a little over a century old. The old parish church is full of historic interest including an ancient "bread charity" cupboard and tombs of the Throckmortons.

If you now wish to cut short your walk, the bus can be picked up near the ancient base of the cross—once used by travellers into the dense Forest of Arden at which to pray for a safe journey—on the A435. The bus halts here on the way back to Studley and Birmingham.

To follow the full route, take the lane beside Coughton Court down to the picturesque spot where it fords the River Arrow. A high footbridge will carry the walker over. Then follow the fieldpath alongside the water, passing the back of the Court with the trees of Timms Grove on our right to come out at Spernall where we can retrace our earlier path back to Studley.

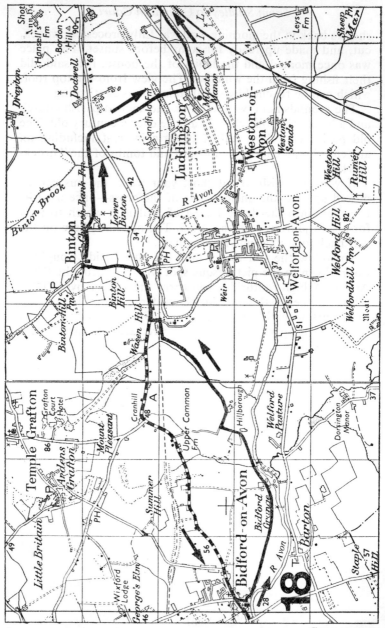

Crown copyright

FROM BIDFORD TO HILLBOROUGH

By train or Midland Red to Stratford. Refreshments at Bidford.

WHAT BETTER, on a clear day than to explore some of the countryside Shakespeare knew so well, all of it within relatively easy reach of the Midlands? So, on this ramble, let us visit the beautiful and ancient manor house closely associated with him—Hillborough Manor.

This could be either a two-car ramble with one car left at Stratford-upon-Avon and the other at Bidford-on-Avon, or by bus for Midland Red buses serve both places and there is a good train service to Stratford from Birmingham.

We start our walk at Bidford where Shakespeare, in a drinking bout at the Falcon Inn—the building still stands although it is no longer an inn—caught the cold which ultimately caused his death. A cafe beside the ancient bridge through the uneven arches of which flows Shakespeare's Avon will possibly induce us to pause to gaze out from its windows on the river, now happily widened and cleared so that it is navigable.

The best and oldest part of Bidford lies east of the church and we set off through this to enjoy the varied architecture in blue lias stone before picking up the signposted fieldpath running along the 30mts. contour line above the river which will bring us to the mill and Bidford Grange.

Skirting a small orchard, a wooden footbridge spans the small stream feeding off the fields into the Avon. Over the high meadows the path continues to West Hillborough, a lovely old stone farmhouse. At this point we can follow the farm road to our left to soon swing right and then reach Hillborough Manor with its dovecote—"Haunted Hillborough" of the Shakespeare jingle.

This ancient building which was carefully repaired a few years ago and is in private hands, was once the residence of Anne Whateley. She was a wealthy and beautiful woman, formerly a Sister of the Order of St. Clare, highly educated, and extensively travelled. She is also supposed to have had a knowledge of several languages. Legend has it that Shakespeare, as a young man, was a frequent visitor and that it was she who provided much of the knowledge and material which enabled him to write as he did.

The story goes that Anne Hathaway whom, of course, Shakespeare married, was then a serving maid at Hillborough. It is true that, on November 27, 1582, a licence was issued at Worcester for the marriage of a William Shakespeare and an Anne Whateley. The following day, however, a bond was issued for the marriage of William Shakespeare to Anne Hathaway.

Leaving this link with history we continue by the fieldpath which follows the brook and skirts the hedge to Blackcliffe and carries us over the bridge spanning the disused railway to the A439. Right along here, take the lane off left to Binton with an interesting church containing the famous Scott window depicting scenes from the ill-fated Antarctic expedition. Scott died in 1912, and he used to stay at Binton. The church was largely rebuilt in 1875 but it contains a 15th century font and old coffin lids.

Swinging right to Lower Binton, pick up the fieldpath which carries over the Ouse Brook and bends down to A439 to pick up another right-of-way over rising ground, crosses the disused railway by farm bridge and, via the farm, drops into Luddington where, according to legend, Shakespeare was married. The church records, however, were lost in a fire and this cannot be verified.

Opposite the farm a fieldpath sign points down to the Avon and a long and lovely path along its bank which, via footbridges and skirting in places, riverside gardens, touches Stratford Racecourse, penetrates beneath the railway and leads into Stratford where meals can readily be obtained. The end of this walk is illustrated on Map 10.

The whole walk covers almost 10 miles but to cut it down to some 4½ miles, return from Blackcliffe to Bidford-on-Avon by the A439, a pleasant main road with wide grass verges and some fine views.

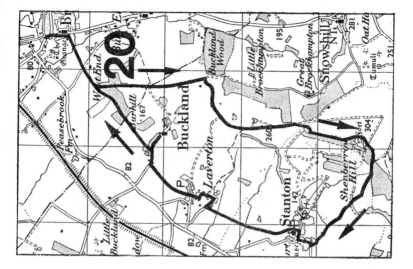

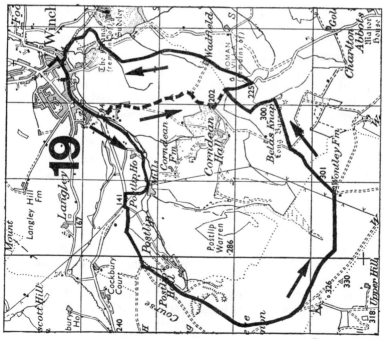

Crown copyright

A COTSWOLD RAMBLE

By car to Winchcombe (1 hour). Refreshments in Winchcombe.

No BOOK of Midland walks would be complete without a good "canter" round the Cotswolds, those lovely hills where even the casual fossil hunter can be sure of coming home with a rucksack heavy with ancient relics. The Romans when they invaded, found this area much to their liking for it resembled their native Italy being warm, and able to grow the grape. Indeed, there are still traces of the "shelves" on the hills where vines were planted. And, to this day, descendents of the large edible snail, which Rome introduced, make their leisured way along the dry-stone walls.

To cover the whole of the Cotswold area would take more than this present book but this walk will give you a good insight to the delights of the area and, if you do all of it, show you many places of interest. To our starting point, Winchcombe, is best reached by car for there is a good free car park here where the car can be left. The car journey should not take much more than an hour from Birmingham.

Having parked, there are cafes in Winchcombe dispensing delectable coffee and buttered scones to send you off refreshed for your day on the Wold.

But first examine a few of the interesting things Winchcombe has to offer, spread out along the little River Isbourne. Once Capital of the Saxon Kingdom of Mercia and later the object of many pilgrims, both to Winchcombe Abbey, founded in 798 A.D. and later sacked by the Danes in 985 A.D., but also the great Abbey of Hailes nearby with its legend of possessing a phial containing a drop of the Blood of Christ. Indeed, the George Inn, with its courtyard balconies, which was a favourite place of call for the pilgrims, is alone worth a visit.

Winchcombe also has some well-preserved stocks and a great church containing an altar frontal cloth from the needle of one of Henry VIII's wives, Katherine of Aragon. The church is famous for a corbel table of grotesque stone heads. It has a collection of encaustic tiles, a fine rood screen and a massive parish chest.

Follow the A46, passing some beautiful Cotswold dwellings, to take the lane off left, signposted to Brockhampton and climb the stile which is signposted as a public footpath to Cleeve Common. You will have the brook on your left for company until you come to the mill where you swing right along the mill road to return to the A46. Left, along here, the main road is soon left to follow the well-defined, climbing track which later, through a gate, leads on to the Common.

This great expanse of high Wold is riddled with tracks but follow the one descending to the left and you will have the beauty of the woodland of Postlip Warren over to your left. The route is easy to follow and passes between the fossil-laden hills.

Out by a little pool, fed by a streamlet which emerges from under the hills, swing right and cross the brook but follow it to the point where it disappears then start a steady climb towards the radio masts. Here bear left over the Wold to drop to Wontley Farm, considered to be one of the most remote in the Cotswolds.

Through the farmyard and left, follow the farm road until the signpost is reached pointing off right to Belas Knap.

This cunningly preserved long barrow is truly a visual link with history. Erected as a "house of the dead" almost 4,000 years ago, when opened, the inner chamber contained 14 skeletons of folk of all ages, squatting on flat stones round the walls. Many more skeletons were found in the outer chambers of this great mound, possibly those of folk sacrificed at the time the principal burials took place. Remains of a fire, flint instruments and animal bones were also unearthed. Here we have a splendid example of the Late Stone Age.

The Barrow has been restored with its dry-stone walling, entrance chambers and great grassy mound, to its original appearance and looks just as it did those thousands of years ago, on this lonely spot, 1000 feet above sea level.

Over a stone stile, follow the high fieldpath to the left with the woodland of Humblebee How on our right. How is a Saxon word indicating a ridge of land and the word Knap from Belas Knap has strong relationship with a Norse word meaning a button or domed object.

There can be few fieldpaths with better views than this and suddenly a glimpse of far-off Winchcombe can be had, spread along the valley of the Isbourne. The path drops through the trees and comes out on the lane opposite one of the wooden signposts marking the Cotswold Way.

Follow the lane to the right until a public right-of-way sign is reached pointing toward Winchcombe. This leads past Humblebee Farm and, through a gate, make for the nearby coppice which houses a building erected over what remains of a Roman villa, the mosaic floor being all that is left.

Continue along the right-of-way to pass Wadfield House with its lovely stone pillars and great gates. Soon you will see, over to the right, the stately beauty of Sudeley Castle, once home of Katherine Parr whom Henry VIII married when he was bloated, fat and 52 years old, and whom she survived. The place, at times open to the public, contains much of historic interest.

Our path comes out beside the Gatehouse and you follow the lane to the left, over the bridge under which flows the Isbourne, to return to Winchcombe.

The whole distance is 8 miles but, if you wish for a shorter walk, including Belas Knap, follow the lane where we left the A46 originally—it is signposted to Belas Knap—and return to Winchcombe from there by taking the route I have described. This will cover some 4 miles.

A RAMBLE ROUND BROADWAY

By car from Birmingham. (1 hour) or bus via Evesham. Refreshments at the Mount Inn, Stanton.

IN EVERYTHING but name, Broadway is a part of the terrain and architecture of Gloucestershire but, probably because the monks of Pershore Abbey in Worcestershire held much property there, it was kept in Worcestershire when the boundaries were drawn. The beautiful town is a Mecca to tourists from all over the world. Indeed, some of the shopkeepers in Broadway are as familiar with foreign currencies as they are with our own metric pound.

And Broadway, realising their value, provides several car parks which are usually well used at all times of the year. The start is more conveniently reached by car and, if you come from Birmingham, the drive should not take you much more than one hour. It is possible to use a bus, however, by journeying by the hourly service from Birmingham to Evesham and connecting with the bus from there to Broadway.

Taking the road due south signposted to Snowshill, you very soon, opposite the church, follow the fieldpath sign pointing to Buckland. Through a kissing-gate the path runs to cross a stream and climb the steep meadows. Over the lane near West End, the path continues to swing left, for a waymarked track, through the woods, but, before you plunge into the trees, pause to look back on the steep, limestone tiled roofs of Broadway, sheltered by the hills.

Through quiet wooded ways the route runs to emerge onto a high meadow. Over this you come to a fenced and well-defined bridleway off left signposted to Shenberrow Hill.

These ancient bridleways, running over the hills are easy to follow, often much easier than fieldpaths for they are, in places, worn below the level of the surrounding fields by the constant passage in times past of cattle, sheep and farm waggons. Even the limestone outcrops are worn down where they occur.

Leaving the fencing and over the high fields, the views to be enjoyed are worth the occasional pause. The hills are capped by trees, many of them magnificent beeches and, although every season has its own delights, autumn with the colouration of the leaf, is my favourite time for this walk. The dry-stone walling is intriguing, constructed by the careful selection of the stone, and entirely without the use of mortar.

Passing the hill fort on Shenberrow Hill, bear right to pick up the track dropping down to Stanton, the distant homesteads of which, all built of the local limestone brought from the long-disused nearby quarries and tiled with the same material, can be seen through the trees. Finally, a steep and muddy track, through a gate, drops out beside the Mount Inn where food and drink can be obtained.

Stanton, contains much of interest and is a village that has been well preserved. Do not miss the old Church of St. Michael which has a tiny muniment room, approached from a door in the nave and climbed to by crumbling stone steps. It contains relics of past times. Examine the old pews at the rear of the nave and you will find the "poppy" heads grooved by the chains of the shepherd's dogs which were tethered here during service.

The Manor of Stanton was given to Winchcombe Abbey by the Saxon Kenulf and it passed, at the Dissolution, to Katherine Parr, given to her by Henry VIII.

Take the path through the churchyard to follow a high yew hedge off left and come out, via a steel gate, on to the meadows, usually white with the sheep which once provided the wealth from which many of the churches were erected. The fieldpath drops onto the lane just below Laverton and here turn right and then left to tread the ways through this charming hamlet where there is a wealth of fine domestic architecture and where, in due season, the cottage gardens are a blaze of colour.

A well-defined bridleway awaits straight ahead and brings the walker out on the lane to Buckland which is followed to the right to inspect what must be one of the finest old churches in the district. Dedicated to St. Michael—usually an indication of there once having been a pagan temple hereabouts—much of the church is Early English and Perpendicular. There are the remains of Rood Loft steps. The font and painted glass in the east window are of 15th century and William Morris was so struck with the beauty of the glass that he paid for the re-leading. It once represented the seven sacraments but now only traces of three can be made out—Confirmation, Matrimony and Extreme Unction.

Buckland church is famous for its so-called Bridal Bowl of maple and silver, made in 1507, which can be examined in its case. Examine, too, the altar frontal on the wall, made from parts of three mass vestments and beautifully embroidered. It contains a "rebus" of William Whytchurch, Abbot of Hailes, in the shape of a white church with the pinnacle of a Monstrance denoting the Holy Blood of Hailes.

Do not miss the painted fragments of stone on the window sill at the rear of the nave. These were probably once part of a reredos in Hailes Abbey.

Buckland gets its name from "Bookland" (manor held by charter or "book") and, remote at the foot of the hills, it kept many ancient Saxon customs, for as late as 1266, there were still no free men in the manor. It was given by the King of Mercia in 709 A.D. to Edburga, Abess of St. Peter's, Gloucester.

Go back a little from the church and pick up the narrow lane on the opposite side. Over a brook through a gate, this is the right-of-way and is waymarked. Up the steep meadows to the trees, the way continues through the woodland where there are many old elder bushes, and, emerging on the pasture, the fieldpath back to Broadway, as per the initial part of this walk, is taken to complete some 8 miles afoot. To shorten the walk to 4 miles, after leaving Buckland Wood, follow the bridleway striking off right which will bring out at Laverton and return to Broadway from there, including a visit to Buckland church.